EXCELLENT SCIENCE EXPERIMENTS

Experiments with MATTER and MATERIALS

Chris Oxlade

Consultant: John Farndon

PowerKiDS press

Published in 2015 by **The Rosen Publishing Group, Inc.**
29 East 21st Street, New York, NY 10010

Library of Congress Cataloging-in-Publication Data

Oxlade, Chris.
Experiments with matter and materials / by Chris Oxlade.
p. cm. — (Excellent science experiments)
Includes index.
ISBN 978-1-4777-5970-7 (pbk.)
ISBN 978-1-4777-5971-4 (6-pack)
ISBN 978-1-4777-5969-1 (library binding)
1. Matter — Properties — Experiments — Juvenile literature.
I. Oxlade, Chris. II. Title.
QC173.36 O95 2015
530—d23

© 2015 Miles Kelly Publishing

Publishing Director: Belinda Gallagher
Creative Director: Jo Cowan
Editors: Amanda Askew, Claire Philip
Editorial Assistant: Lauren White
Designers: Joe Jones, Kayleigh Allen
Cover Designer: Simon Lee

Photographer: Simon Pask
Production Manager: Elizabeth Collins
Reprographics: Stephan Davis, Thom Allaway,
Anthony Cambray, Jennifer Hunt,
Lorraine King

ACKNOWLEDGEMENTS
The publishers would like to thank the following sources for the use of their photographs:
Shutterstock.com Cover Ohn Mar; 7(tr) Sean Gladwell, (c) Brian A Jackson, (br) travis
manley, (bl) fatbob; 11(c) Yobidaba, (tr) AdamEdwards, (br) Rtimages. Every effort has
been made to acknowledge the source and copyright holder of each picture. Miles Kelly
Publishing apologies for any unintentional errors or omissions.unintentional errors or
omissions.

Printed in the United States of America

CPSIA Compliance Information: Batch CW15PK: For Further Information contact Rosen Publishing, New York, New York at 1-800-237-9932

CONTENTS

A material can be described by its properties, such as its color or strength.

Experiment time!

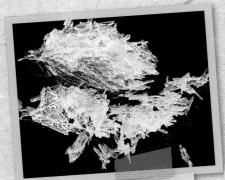

What shape are salt crystals? Find out on page 13.

Do oil and water mix? Find out on page 16.

Help needed

Help and hazards

- All of the experiments are suitable for younger readers to conduct, but you will need help and supervision with some. This is usually because the experiment requires the use of a stove or oven, a knife or scissors, or food coloring. These experiments are marked with a "Help needed" symbol.

- Read the instructions together with an adult before starting, and have an adult help to assemble the equipment and supervise the experiment.

- It may be useful for an adult to do a risk assessment to avoid any possible hazards before you begin. Check that long hair and any loose clothing are tied back

- Also check that materials such as bleach are disposed of safely, and that the oven is turned off after use.

What is MATTER?

Matter makes up everything you can see, from the water in your glass, to the chair you are sitting on. It also makes up some things you cannot see, such as the air you breathe. There are three states of matter, which make up nearly every substance in the Universe.

The three states of matter

Everything around us is either a solid, liquid, or gas, made up of billions of units called atoms. Atoms are some of the smallest objects that exist, and are invisible. Two or more atoms joined together make up a molecule. Groups of molecules make up a substance.

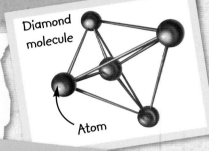

Diamond molecule

Atom

Changing state

A substance can change from one state to another by gaining or losing energy, in the form of heat.

Solid

Atoms or molecules in a solid cannot move. They are tightly packed together, so they keep their shape and feel firm.

If a liquid is cooled, it turns into a solid. This is called freezing.

If a solid is heated, it turns into a liquid. This is called melting.

Liquid

In a liquid, atoms or molecules can move or flow, but they stay the same distance apart. The links between the molecules are weaker than in a solid. A liquid can flow and fill the shape of its container.

If a gas is cooled, it turns into a liquid. This is called condensing.

If a liquid is heated, it turns into a gas. This is called evaporation.

Gas

Atoms or molecules in a gas move quickly and in all directions. The molecules bounce around because the forces between them are not strong enough to keep them together.

What are MATERIALS?

Every *substance* is made from a material, or a combination of materials. A material's properties, such as strength or flexibility (bendiness), make it useful for different things. Modern materials can be natural, or synthetic (chemically man-made).

Natural resources

Since ancient times, a large number of everyday materials have been made from plants, such as cotton and wood. Natural materials such as these need to be recycled (made into new things) and reused, so they do not run out.

Wood

There are many different types of wood, varying in strength, color, and weight. Wood comes from trees and is mainly used for fuel, or in construction (building).

Chair

Rubber bands

Rubber

Natural rubber is made from milky sap, called latex, found in some tropical trees. However, it can also be made synthetically. Rubber is flexible, tough, and waterproof, which makes it useful for making car tires.

Synthetic substances

Plastic, steel, and glass are examples of synthetic materials. Sometimes a mixture of both natural and synthetic materials can be used – for example in clothing.

Plastic drinking bottle

Plastic

Waterproof, long-lasting, and strong, this synthetic material is mainly made from substances found in petroleum (crude oil). Plastics can be easily shaped and molded and are used in many everyday products.

Rope

5

Polyester

This synthetic material is often used to make clothing, as it dries quickly and holds its shape well. Rope is also often made from polyester because it is very strong.

USING this book

Each experiment has numbered instructions and clear explanations about your findings. Read through all the instructions before you start an experiment, and then follow them carefully, one at a time. If you are not sure what to do, ask an adult.

Experiment symbols

① Shows how long the experiment will take, once you have collected all the equipment you need.

② Shows if you need to ask an adult to help you with the experiment.

③ Shows how easy or difficult the experiment is to do.

SALTY to freshwater

Can you separate the salt and water in salty water? Yes, by distillation – try this experiment to see how.

①	②	③
30 min	Help needed	Tricky

You will need

- work surface
- stove
- water
- glass
- table salt
- teaspoon
- small dish
- saucepan
- aluminum foil
- ice cubes
- jug

Introduction
See what you will be learning about in each experiment.

Things you will need
You should be able to find the equipment around the house or from a supermarket. No special equipment is needed. Always ask before using materials from home.

⚠️ ### Safety
If there is a "Help needed" symbol at the start of the experiment, you must ask an adult to help you.

The warning symbol also tells you to be careful when using knives or scissors, or heat. Always ask an adult for help.

ⓐ Half fill a glass with water. Add four teaspoons of salt and stir to make the salt dissolve. This is the salty solution.

ⓑ Pour most of the salty water into a saucepan. Then stand a small dish in the center.
There should be no water in this dish

ⓒ Put a piece of aluminum foil over the top of the pan. Gently press down the center of the foil slightly to make a dip. Put a few ice cubes in the dip.

20

Stages
Numbers and letters guide you through the stages of each experiment.

6

Doing the experiments

⭐ Clear a surface to work on, such as a table, and cover it with newspaper if you need to.

⭐ You could wear an apron or an old t-shirt to protect your clothing.

⭐ Gather all the equipment you need before you start, and tidy up after each experiment.

⭐ Ask an adult to help you when an experiment is marked with a "Help needed" or warning symbol.

⭐ Work over a tray or sink when you are pouring water.

⭐ Always ask an adult to help you if you are unsure what to do.

Explanation
At the end of each experiment is a question-and-answer explanation. It tells you what should have happened and why.

Put the pan on the stove and heat it very gently. Allow the water to boil for a few minutes (but make sure all the solution does not boil away). Be careful as the water will get hot.

Q Do the waters taste different?

A Yes, the water in the dish is fresh water – free of salt. The water evaporated (turned to steam), leaving the salt behind in the pan, but the steam condensed (turned to water) on the cold foil and the water dripped into the dish. This process is called distillation and it is used to get fresh water from seawater.

Make sure the dish is cold before you touch it

Remove the saucepan from the stove and leave it for one hour to cool completely. Then remove the foil. There should now be water in the dish. Taste the water in the pan and the water in the dish.

Also try...

In the experiment on distillation, you removed the salt from the water and kept the water.

If you just want to keep the salt, put a saucer of the salty water in a warm place. The water will slowly evaporate, leaving the salt behind.

Also try...
Simple mini-experiments test the science you've learned.

21

7

Labels
Handy labels will provide you with useful tips and information to help your experiment run smoothly.

Scientist KIT

Before you begin experimenting you will need to gather some equipment. You should be able to find all of it around the house or from a local supermarket. Ask an adult's permission before using anything and take care when you see a warning sign.

From the craft box

- adhesive tape
- colored pencils
- felt-tip pens (water soluble)
- lead pencils
- pencil sharpener
- thick card stock
- thin card stock

Pencils

Card stock

From the kitchen

- aluminum foil
- chopping board
- colander
- funnel
- glasses
- jars
- jug
- knife
- large plastic bowl
- paper towel
- saucepan with lid
- saucers
- scissors
- small dish
- sieve
- tablespoons
- teaspoons
- thermometer
- wooden spoon

Scissors

Handy hint!
Ice cubes and frozen peas will melt very quickly. Leave them in the freezer until you are ready to use them.

Ice cubes

Funnel

Foody things

- baking soda
- cooking oil
- flour
- food coloring
- ice cubes
- lemon juice
- milk
- peas
- red cabbage
- table salt
- tea bag
- vinegar
- water

⚠️ Warning!
Scissors and knives are extremely sharp and can cut you easily. Make sure you ask an adult for help. When passing scissors or a knife, always point the handle towards the other person.

Tea bag

Other stuff

- 9V battery
- balloon
- Epsom salts
- filter paper
- household bleach
- petroleum jelly
- short sticks
- small plastic water bottle

Petroleum jelly

Balloons

⚠ Warning!
Bleach can be dangerous if not used correctly. Ask an adult for help and if you get any on your skin, be sure to wash it off immediately with water.

Places you'll need to work

- fridge
- stovetop
- oven
- work surface

⚠ Warning!
Be careful not to burn yourself on the stove. Remember it is hot enough to cook food on! Ask an adult for help.

Remember to recycle and reuse

One way to help the environment is by recycling and reusing materials such as glass, paper, plastic, and scrap metals. It is mostly cheaper and less wasteful than making new products from scratch.

Reusing means you use materials again in their original form rather than throwing them away.

Recycling is when materials are taken to a plant where they can be melted and remade into either the same or new products.

Peas

Handy hint!
Plastic bottles come in many different colors. Try to use a clear bottle so that you can see your experiment working.

9

ICE TO
water to steam

Ice, liquid water, and steam are just water, but in solid, liquid, and gas forms. Solids, liquids, and gases are the three states of matter. This experiment shows that water has different properties in each of the three states.

15 min   Help needed   Easy

You will need

- stove
- saucepan with lid
- wooden spoon
- ice cubes
- thermometer that measures from 32°F to 212°F (0°C to 100°C)

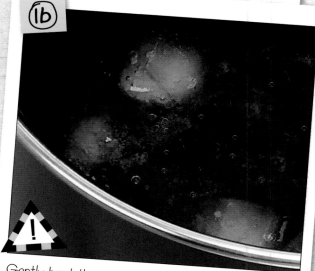

1b

Gently heat the saucepan and stir the ice. Ask an adult to help you heat the water on the stove because it will become hot. When the ice has begun to melt, test the temperature of the water with the thermometer.

1a

Put a saucepan on the stove and cover the bottom of the saucepan with ice cubes. Press on the ice cubes with the wooden spoon and watch what happens.

Q Does the ice flow?

A **No, at first the solid ice doesn't flow or change shape.** As the temperature of the water rises, it changes state – from solid ice to liquid water. This change from solid to liquid is called melting, and for ice, it normally happens at 32°F (0°C).

2a Keep heating and melting the ice until you have liquid water. Look at how the liquid is different from the solid.

3 Extreme steam!

Soon you will see bubbles forming – the liquid water is turning to steam. Put a lid on the pan and turn off the heat before all the water is gone. You should have a pan full of steam. Don't touch the pan as the steam will be very hot.

2b Turn up the heat. Ask an adult to help you test the temperature again to see if it has changed.

Q What does the steam do?

A The steam fills the saucepan. If you were to remove the lid, it would escape. The liquid water has changed to steam. This change of state is called boiling. For water, it normally happens at 212°F (100°C).

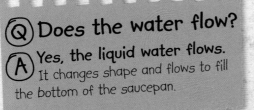

Q Does the water flow?

A Yes, the liquid water flows. It changes shape and flows to fill the bottom of the saucepan.

CREATE
crystals

Have you ever looked really closely at table salt or sugar? If so, you've already seen crystals. Here's how to grow some crystals of your own.

15 min preparation 3 days for results

Help needed

Hard

You will need

- work surface
- oven
- fridge
- table salt
- Epsom salts
- 2 glasses
- jug
- 2 teaspoons
- 4 saucers
- water
- optional: food coloring

Preparation

Half fill two glasses with warm water. Add a few teaspoons of table salt to one glass and a few teaspoons of Epsom salts to the other glass. Stir the water in each glass so that the salts dissolve. These are your salt solutions. You could add a few drops of food coloring for fun.

1a

Don't add too much solution to the water

Pour a little table salt solution onto two saucers. Leave one saucer in a warm place. Examine the crystals after one hour, then at regular intervals for about three days.

1b

Ask an adult to put the other saucer in the oven at 275°F (140°C) for about 15 minutes or until all the water has evaporated. Carefully remove the crystals from the oven and examine them.

Q What shape are the crystals?

A **The table salt crystals look like cubes.** They are called cubic crystals. In the solution you made, the tiny particles of table salt were mixed with water. As the water evaporated in the air or oven, the particles joined together to make crystals. Crystals have straight edges and flat faces because the particles are arranged in a neat, regular way.

Crystals formed in a warm place

After 3 days

Crystals formed in the oven

After 15 minutes

2a

Pour some Epsom salt solution onto two saucers. Put one saucer in a warm place and examine the crystals at regular intervals for a few days.

2b

Put the other saucer in the fridge. Examine the crystals after 10 minutes, 30 minutes and one hour.

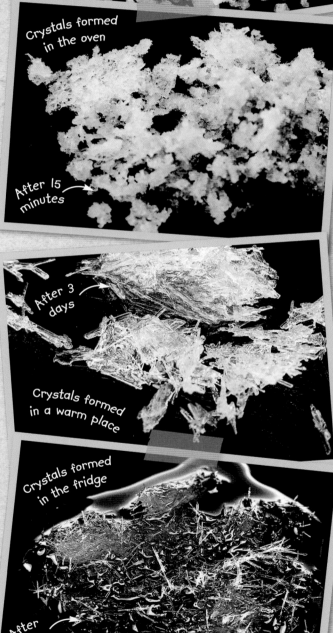

After 3 days

Crystals formed in a warm place

Crystals formed in the fridge

After 1 hour

Q Are the Epsom salt crystals different?

A **Yes, the Epsom salt crystals are needle shaped.** Just like the cubic crystals, they have straight edges and flat faces.

Mixing like MAGIC

Materials are made of millions of tiny particles. This experiment shows that in a liquid, the particles are constantly jiggling and moving.

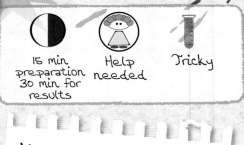

15 min preparation 30 min for results

Help needed

Tricky

You will need

- work surface
- petroleum jelly
- 2 clean, empty jars
- food coloring
- water
- spoon
- jug
- piece of thin card stock
- large plastic bowl

a

Make the jelly really thick

Smear plenty of petroleum jelly around the rims of the two jars to make a watertight seal.

c

Fill the other jar with water, right to the top, too.

b

Half fill one of the jars with water, add a few drops of food coloring and stir. Then fill the jar with water, right to the brim.

d

Make the card stock 1 inch bigger than the jar

Cut a square of thin card stock, large enough to cover the opening of one of the jars. Put the card stock on top of the jar with colored water in it.

14

e

The openings of the jars need to line up so the water doesn't leak out

Place the jar of clear water in a large plastic bowl. With one hand supporting the card stock, carefully turn over the jar of colored water. Slowly slip out your hand and place the top jar on the bottom jar. You might need some help with this. Leave the jars to settle for 10 minutes before moving on to step f.

f

While holding the top jar steady, slowly and carefully slide out the card stock. Again, you might need some help with this step.

Dark red... lighter... light red!

Clear... darker... light red!

After 1 minute

After 10 minutes

After 30 minutes

Q What happens to the colored water?

A It mixes with the clear water. The tiny water molecules are tightly packed together and are constantly moving. The water molecules from the two jars slowly mix together, carrying the particles of food coloring with them.

Can you MIX IT?

Many materials are made by mixing other materials. In these experiments, you'll put two different materials in the same container to see that some mix well and others don't mix at all.

15 min   No help needed   Easy

You will need
- work surface
- 5 jars
- cooking oil
- water
- 5 spoons
- table salt
- flour

①

Put some water and cooking oil into a jar and stir with a spoon.

Q Do oil and water mix?

A No matter how much you stir, the oil and water don't mix. After stirring, they quickly separate again, leaving a layer of oil on top of the water. This is because the particles of oil and the particles of water repel each other.

②

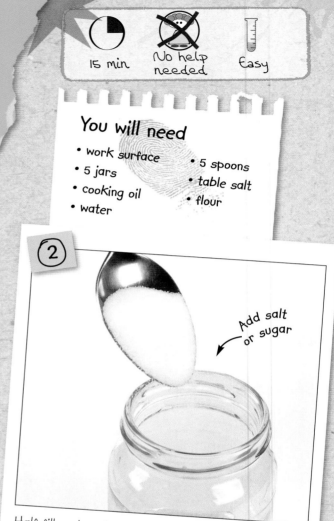

Add salt or sugar

Half fill a clean jar with water, add a spoonful of salt and stir.

Q Do salt and water mix?

A Yes, when you mix salt with water, the salt seems to disappear. In fact, it dissolves – it breaks into tiny particles that mix with the water. The mixture is called a solution.

16

③ Use a clean jar and mix a spoonful of flour into half a jar of water.

Q Do flour and water mix?

A **Yes, flour and water mix.** Unlike oil and water, flour mixes much better and forms a paste. This is because the water and flour do not repel each other.

Goooey!

④ Pour some cooking oil into a clean jar. Add a few pinches of salt to the oil and stir.

⑤ Half fill a clean jar with water, add five spoonfuls of salt and stir. Add another five spoonfuls and keep stirring.

Add as much salt as possible

Q How much salt will dissolve?

A **Lots!** Eventually you will not be able to make any more salt disappear into the water. There are no water particles free to break up any more salt.

Q Do oil and salt mix?

A **No, the salt does not dissolve.** Instead it just sinks to the bottom. This is because the oil does not break up the salt crystals like water does.

Leftover salt

17

SPLITTING the mix

A mixture is made up of two or more different materials mixed together. Sometimes you may want to separate the materials in a mixture.

30 min | No help needed | Hard

You will need

- work surface
- 3 clean, empty jars
- water
- teaspoon
- tea bag
- table salt
- peas (frozen or fresh, not canned)
- colander
- large plastic bowl
- paper towel or filter paper

Preparation

Half fill three jars with water. Add some frozen or fresh peas to the first jar. Add the tea leaves from a tea bag to the second jar. Stir two teaspoons of salt into the third jar.

①

Place a colander over a large plastic bowl. Pour half the mixture of water and peas into the colander.

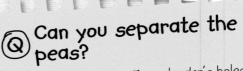

Q Can you separate the peas?

A Yes, you can. The colander's holes are small enough to trap the peas.

Pour half the mixture of tea leaves and water through the colander, and then half the mixture of salt and water.

Put a piece of paper towel in the colander. Pour the rest of the tea and water mixture through.

Q Can you separate tea or salt?
A No, they both stay with the water. The colander's holes are too large to trap tea leaves or salt particles.

Use clean paper towel

Put a new piece of paper towel in the colander. Pour the rest of the salt and water mixture through the paper. Dip your finger in the water and taste it.

Q Does a filter stop the tea leaves?
A Yes, it does. The paper towel has very small holes between the paper fibers. They are small enough to trap the tea leaves, but not the water.

Q Can you filter salt from water?
A No, the filter paper lets salt water through. This is why the water tastes salty. The particles of salt water are extremely tiny and easily pass through the holes.

SALTY to freshwater

Can you separate the salt and water in salty water? Yes, by distillation – try this experiment to see how.

30 min   Help needed   Tricky

You will need

- work surface
- stove
- water
- glass
- table salt
- teaspoon
- small dish
- saucepan
- aluminum foil
- ice cubes
- jug

a

Half fill a glass with water. Add four teaspoons of salt and stir to make the salt dissolve. This is the salty solution.

b

There should be no water in this dish

Pour most of the salty water into a saucepan. Then stand a small dish in the center.

c

Put a piece of aluminum foil over the top of the pan. Gently press down the center of the foil slightly to make a dip. Put a few ice cubes in the dip.

20

(d)

Put the pan on the stove and heat it very gently. Allow the water to boil for a few minutes (but make sure all the solution does not boil away). Be careful as the water will get hot.

(e)

Make sure the dish is cold before you touch it

Remove the saucepan from the stove and leave it for one hour to cool completely. Then remove the foil. There should now be water in the dish. Taste the water in the pan and the water in the dish.

Do the waters taste different?

A **Yes, the water in the dish is fresh water – free of salt.** The water evaporated (turned to steam), leaving the salt behind in the pan, but the steam condensed (turned to water) on the cold foil and the water dripped into the dish. This process is called distillation and it is used to get fresh water from seawater.

Also try...

In the experiment on distillation, you removed the salt from the water and kept the water.

If you just want to keep the salt, put a saucer of the salty water in a warm place. The water will slowly evaporate, leaving the salt behind.

COLOR
separation

Inks, food coloring and dyes are often mixtures containing different colors called pigments. Try this experiment to separate pigments so that you can see what they are.

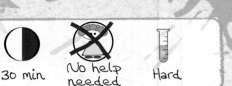

30 min   No help needed   Hard

You will need

- work surface
- 4 strips of filter paper, 1 in. × 4 in.
- water
- 4 clean, empty jars
- 4 pencils or short sticks
- adhesive tape
- 4 water-soluble felt-tip pens or food coloring
- scissors
- water
- jug

(a)

Wrap a strip of filter paper around each of your four pencils, so the paper is as long as your jar is tall. Stick it to the pencil with sticky tape.

Trim any excess paper

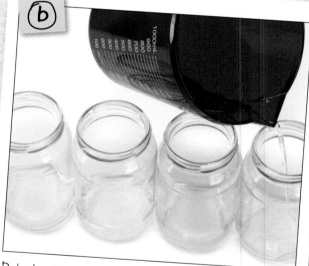

(b)

Put about 1 inch of water in each of the four jars.

(c)

Use plenty of food coloring or ink

About 1 inch from the end of each strip, either draw a large dot with a felt-tip pen or add a drop of food coloring.

(d)

Carefully lower a strip (with the colored dot at the bottom end) into each jar, so the dot is about ½ inch above the water's surface. Examine the paper every ten minutes for an hour.

(A) **The colors spread out and separate.** The filter paper strips soak up the water. The water picks up the different pigments in the ink and carries them upwards through the paper. The water on the paper slowly evaporates, and this draws more water upwards. Different pigments are carried different distances up the paper, and as a result are separated.

After 10 minutes

green = yellow + blue

After 30 minutes

yellow – no change

blue = red + blue

red = yellow + purple

After 60 minutes

23

CABBAGE colors

What links lemon juice and bleach? One is an acid and the other is an alkali. They are opposites. Here's an experiment to show what is acid and what is alkali – using cabbage!

30 min   Help needed   Tricky

You will need

- work surface
- stove
- red cabbage
- knife
- chopping board
- saucepan
- sieve
- 3 clean, empty jars
- large plastic bowl
- teaspoons
- lemon juice
- baking soda
- household bleach
- water

Preparation

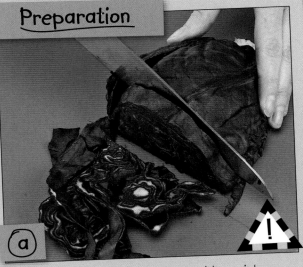

(a) Ask an adult to chop half a red cabbage into small pieces.

(b) Put the pieces of cabbage in a saucepan and cover with water. Ask an adult to bring it to a boil and simmer for five minutes. Turn off the heat and allow the water and cabbage to cool.

(c) Hold a sieve over the large plastic bowl. Pour the cabbage and water through it, so the purple water collects in the bowl.

(d) Half fill the three jars with some of the purple water. The purple color means the liquid is neutral.

① Add a few drops of bleach to the first jar and stir. Ask an adult to help you pour the bleach.

Q What does bleach do to the water?

A It turns the purple water green, then yellow. Bleach is an alkali.

② Put a few drops of lemon juice into the second jar and stir.

Q What does lemon juice do to the water?

A Lemon juice turns the water red. It is an acid.

③ Put a teaspoon of baking soda into the third jar and stir.

Q What does baking soda do to the water?

A It turns the purple color to blue. Baking soda is a chemical called a *base*, which turns water into an alkali. But it is not as alkaline as the bleach.

Bleach — Strong alkali

Lemon — Acid

Baking soda — Weak alkali

By changing color, the cabbage water tells us whether chemicals are acids or alkalis. It is called an indicator.

25

Bubbles AND FROTH

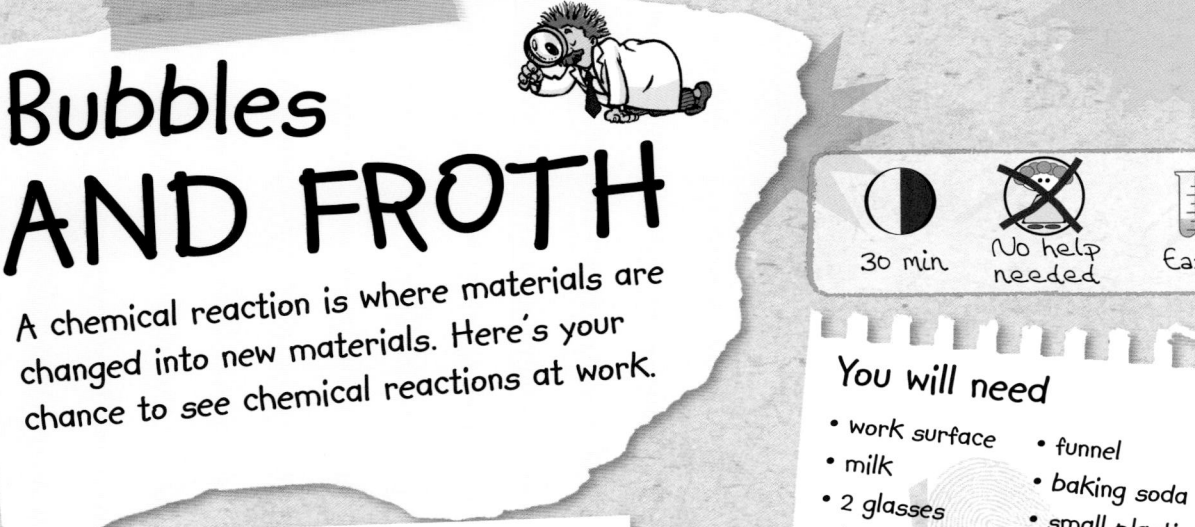

A chemical reaction is where materials are changed into new materials. Here's your chance to see chemical reactions at work.

30 min | No help needed | Easy

You will need

- work surface
- milk
- 2 glasses
- tablespoons
- vinegar
- filter paper
- funnel
- baking soda
- small plastic water bottle
- balloon
- saucer

1a

Put half a cup of milk into a glass and stir in two tablespoons of vinegar. The vinegar will make the milk turn lumpy.

1b

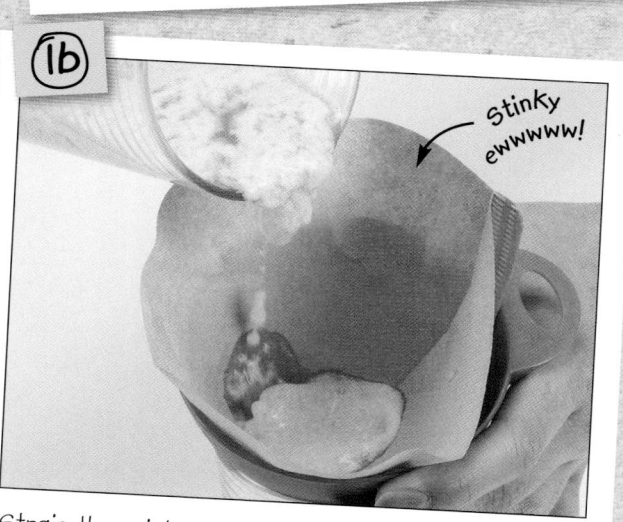

Stinky ewwwww!

Strain the mixture through filter paper into another glass. You don't need to keep the liquid.

1c

After an hour or two, remove the pasty substance from the paper onto a saucer.

Q What do vinegar and milk make?

A **They make a pasty substance.** A material called casein in the milk reacts with the vinegar to make a new substance, which becomes hard like plastic when it dries.

Touch it, if you dare!

26

2a

Put the narrow part of a funnel into the neck of a balloon. Carefully put two tablespoons of baking soda into the funnel and shake it down into the balloon.

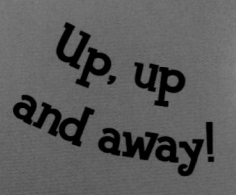

Up, up and away!

2b

Don't tip any baking soda into the bottle yet

Add 1 inch of vinegar to the bottle. Then carefully attach the balloon to the top of the bottle.

2c

Lift up the balloon and shake it so the baking soda falls into the bottle.

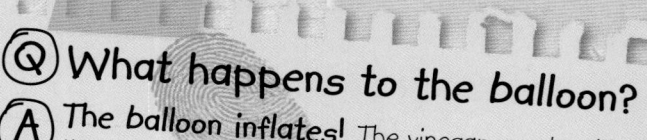

Q **What happens to the balloon?**

A **The balloon inflates!** The vinegar reacts with the baking soda, making carbon dioxide gas. This gas fills the balloon.

27

ELECTRIC bubble maker

In this experiment you send electricity through water. The electricity breaks up the water, making tiny bubbles of gas.

30 min   No help needed   Hard

You will need
- work surface
- thick card stock
- clean, empty jar
- 2 lead pencils, the same length
- pencil sharpener
- water
- 9V battery

a Cut a square of thick card stock about 1 inch wider than the opening of the jar.

b Sharpen both ends of the pencils. Then carefully push the pencils through the card stock, about 1 inch apart.

c Don't let the pencils touch the bottom

Half fill the jar with water. Then place the card stock on top of the jar and slide the pencils up or down so that their ends are level and underwater.

28

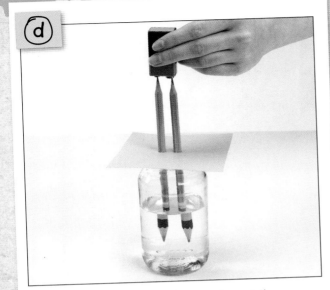

d

Hold the battery upside down on top of the pencils so that the battery terminals touch the pencil leads.

Add some salt to the water, stir it in and repeat the experiment. Sniff the air above the jar.

Can you smell chlorine or a "swimming pool" smell? When you add salt, chlorine comes from the pencil lead attached to the positive terminal. Chlorine is one of the elements in salt (which is sodium chloride, or NaCl).

pop!
pop!
pop!

bubbly

Q Can you see bubbles?

A The small bubbles that appear on the pencil leads and rise to the surface are bubbles of oxygen and hydrogen. These are the two chemical elements in water. Oxygen is produced when the pencil lead touches the positive battery terminal, and hydrogen is made when the pencil lead touches the negative battery terminal.

Quiz ZONE

Get ready to test how much you've learned from the experiments in this book. Write down your answers on a piece of paper and then check them against the answers on page 31. No cheating!

Q1 picture clue

What is the missing word?

 If water is heated, it starts to change from a liquid to a _____ .

 Instead of throwing away plastic and paper, we should _____ .

 If two substances will not mix, they _____ each other.

 When a gas cools and changes to a liquid, it is _____ .

5 The process of heating water until it evaporates, then cools to become a liquid again, is called _____ .

Remember, remember

6 At what temperature will water begin to boil?

7 When vinegar is added to baking soda, which gas is produced?

8 Which two chemical elements make up water (H_2O)?

9 What shape are table salt crystals?

Q7 picture clue

True or false?

 10 When oil and water are mixed together, the oil dissolves into the water.

 11 Rubber is a natural material.

Q10 picture clue

Multiple choice

 12 When atoms or molecules are tightly packed together, and they cannot move around, what do they form? A solid, liquid, or gas?

 13 What is the name of the process that changes ice to water? Melting, evaporating, or freezing?

 14 Which of these is a natural material? Wood, plastic, or polyester?

 15 What is made when salt and water mix? A solution, a reaction, or a mixture?

Q14 picture clue

What word beginning with...

Q16 picture clue

 16 F turns a liquid into a solid?

 17 A Is the opposite of an alkali?

 18 P make up colors in inks, dyes, and food coloring?

 19 F can be used to separate a solid from a liquid?

 31

quiz answers

1. Gas 2. Recycle 3. Repel 4. Condensing 5. Distillation
6. 212°F (100°C) 7. Carbon dioxide 8. Hydrogen and oxygen
9. Cube shaped 10. False – they repel each other 11. True
12. Solid 13. Melting 14. Wood 15. Solution 16. Freezing
17. Acid 18. Pigments 19. Filter

GLOSSARY

Acid A chemical substance that has a pH level of less than 7.

Alkali A chemical substance that has a pH level of more than 7.

Atom The smallest particle of an element.

Boiling point The temperature at which a liquid bubbles and changes into a gas when it is heated.

Condensing The process of a gas changing to a liquid as it cools.

Dissolving If a solid dissolves, it mixes with a liquid and makes a solution.

Distillation The process used to separate a liquid from a solution by evaporation and condensing.

Element A simple chemical substance that consists of only one kind of atom, and cannot be broken down.

Evaporation The process in which water is heated and changes from a liquid to a gas.

Filter To separate two substances in a mixture by passing it through something, such as a sieve.

Freezing point The temperature at which a liquid cools and changes into a solid.

Material What every substance is made from. Materials can be natural (e.g. wood), or synthetic (e.g. polyester).

Matter All substances are made up of very small particles, or matter, and can be a solid, liquid, or gas.

Melting The process that changes a solid into a liquid, mainly when heated.

Mixture A substance that contains two or more different substances that are mixed, but not chemically bound. They can be easily separated.

Molecule At least two atoms held together by a chemical bond.

Neutral A chemical substance with a pH level equal to 7.

pH scale The measure of how acidic or alkaline a solution is.

Pigment A mixture of different colors that make up one color when put together.

Reaction When a chemical change occurs and materials are changed into new materials. E.g. when vinegar reacts with baking soda, carbon dioxide is made.

Repel When two or more substances do not mix.

Separation When two or more materials in a mixture are moved apart.

Solution A mixture in which a gas, solid or liquid is dissolved in a liquid.

Thermometer A piece of equipment used to measure temperature.

INDEX

WEBSITES

Due to the changing nature of Internet links, PowerKids Press has developed an online list of websites related to the subject of this book. This site is updated regularly. Please use this link to access the list:

www.powerkidslinks.com/ese/matter

2/16

For my family,
who keep me young and continue to
teach me the true meaning of Christmas
—J. S.

For Mom and Dad,
two of the greatest gifts
I have ever received
—H. F.

Henry Holt and Company, *Publishers since 1866*
Henry Holt® is a registered trademark of Macmillan Publishing Group, LLC
120 Broadway, New York, NY 10271 • mackids.com

Library of Congress Cataloging-in-Publication Data is available
ISBN 978-1-250-25561-7

Our books may be purchased in bulk for promotional, educational, or business use.
Please contact your local bookseller or the Macmillan Corporate and Premium Sales Department
at (800) 221-7945 ext. 5442 or by email at MacmillanSpecialMarkets@macmillan.com.

First edition, 2020
The illustrations for this book were created digitally.
Printed in China by Hung Hing Off-set Printing Co. Ltd.,
Heshan City, Guangdong Province

1 3 5 7 9 10 8 6 4 2

SANTA BABY

Jonathan Stutzman
illustrated by Heather Fox

HENRY HOLT AND COMPANY • NEW YORK

THERE WERE ONLY four days until Christmas, and Santa Claus was feeling old.

Santa *was* old, of course;
he had been Santa for hundreds
and hundreds of years.

SUIT
Height:
Waist:
Arms:
Chest:

But this year, his beard
seemed whiter.

His wrinkles,
more wrinkly.

His belly, less jolly
and more . . . jelly.

Every year it was the same—

wrangling the reindeer,

climbing rooftops and chimneys,

lugging and reaching and bending and stooping to deliver
all those presents—and it had taken a toll on Santa.

HO HO

OWW

For the first time in centuries, Santa Claus did not feel the Christmas spirit.

He felt only the ache of his body.

NORTH POLE

Santa tried to be jolly.
But holiday festivities
only made

his feet,

knees,

back,

ears,

face,

and fingers hurt.

Santa was sour and sore, but all the children in the entire world were counting on him. So, he did something he had never done before. He called upon the magic of Christmas . . .

and made a wish.

"Make me young again!"

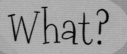

What?

WUMP

Wow!

And younger he grew.

And younger.

And just right!

And . . . too young.

Until . . .

. . . Santa was a baby.

Santa Baby tried to calm the elves. He explained
what happened, then laid out an easy, three-step
plan for how to change himself back to normal.

But all the elves heard was . . .

Christmas was in serious trouble.

HERE WERE THREE DAYS UNTIL
Christmas, and the elves decided to run Santa Baby
through some tests to see which Santa skills he still had. They
started with the ones essential to a successful Christmas:

Driving the sleigh.

Going up and down chimneys.

Delivering gifts.

It was worse than the elves had imagined.

Much,

much

worse.

So, they tried something easier—
they gave Santa Baby his list to check.
But instead of checking it . . .

. . . he chewed his list.
He chewed it twice.

The elves did
not think this
was very nice.
Actually, they
found it quite
naughty.

NAUGHTY OR Nice?

☑ Susan ☒ Walter
☒ Ralphie ☑ Reggie
☒ Kate ☑ Cindy
☑ George ☑ Sam
☑ Dudley ☑ Angel

THERE WERE TWO DAYS

until Christmas, and the elves were desperate. If they were to save Christmas, Santa Baby had to grow up—and *FAST*.

Vegetables! they thought. That would help him grow!

Eat your num-nums!

NO!

But Santa Baby did not want to eat any vegetables.

The only num-nums Santa Baby wanted were cookies.

What about milk? Santa Baby *loved* milk!
But the only thing that grew was his diaper.
Christmas was doomed.

It was Christmas Eve,

and all the elves' ideas had failed. Whispers swirled through the North Pole that Christmas would have to be canceled.

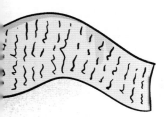

Santa Baby considered giving up. But then he thought about all the children who would wake the next morning with empty stockings and no presents under their trees.

So, Santa Baby stood up and put on his big-boy cap. He knew he had to *try*.

He gathered the elves and laid out another plan.
He spoke slower this time, with great passion, and
used hand-drawn diagrams (for the visual learners).

And then, concentrating his very, *very* hardest, Santa Baby
babbled the three little words he knew would inspire the elves:

Cheers erupted across the North Pole! With renewed hope, the elves sprang into action!

As the clock struck midnight, the elves loaded the final gifts onto the sleigh and buckled Santa Baby into his safety-approved sleigh-seat.

Off like a flash, the sleigh shot into the night.

From house to house they dashed.
The presents were placed,
the stockings were stuffed,
every num-num was eaten.

Everything was going so well—
Santa Baby felt like Santa again!

But then
Santa Baby
stumbled and
tumbled . . .

. . . and
hurried
down the
chimney
in fright.

Santa Baby bumped his bottom and began to cry.

He cried with the fury
of a thousand carolers.

When Santa Baby opened his eyes, a girl was there.

In her hands, she held a gift she had been given on her first Christmas—a gift she cherished more than anything.

A gift she gave to Santa Baby.

In the soft twinkle of tree light,
in the arms of a kind child,
Santa Baby felt the beauty and
wonder of Christmas again, as
if for the first time.

WUMP

And before he knew it—

Santa was Santa again. Merry, old, achy Santa.

His beard
was white.

His wrinkles,
wrinkly.

His belly,
jelly—
but jolly!

In all the Christmases through all the centuries he had lived, Santa had never felt more full of life.

AND AS HE FLEW OFF

into the frosted night, Santa made another wish—not for himself but for everyone.

No matter how young you are or how old you feel, may you experience the wonder of Christmas as if for the first time . . . again and again and again.

Traditional Games of Childhood
Let's play

Kids Can Press Ltd. acknowledges with appreciation
the assistance of the Canada Council and the Ontario
Arts Council in the production of this book.

Canadian Cataloguing in Publication Data

Gryski, Camilla, 1948-
          Let's play : traditional games of childhood

ISBN 1-55074-256-6

1. Games – Juvenile literature. 2. Games – History –
Juvenile literature. I. Petricic, Dusan. II. Title.

GV1203.C79 1995   j796.1   C95–930517–3

Kids Can Press Ltd.
29 Birch Avenue
Toronto, Ontario, Canada
M4V 1E2

Edited by Trudee Romanek

Printed and bound in Hong Kong
by Wing King Tong Company Limited

95 0 9 8 7 6 5 4 3 2 1

Traditional Games of Childhood

Let's play

Illustrated by
DUŠAN PETRIČIĆ

Written by
CAMILLA GRYSKI

KIDS CAN PRESS LTD., TORONTO

To my children Miloš, Gordan, Irena and Miša, for keeping me childish. – D. P.

This book is for my friend Caroline, who still knows how to play. – C. G.

I wish to express my warmest thanks to Professor Ivan Ivić
and Danijela Petrović, both from the Institute for Psychology
at Belgrade's Faculty of Philosophy, and to my friend, Zoran Papić,
for their help and support for the idea for this book in its early,
Belgrade phase. – D.P.

I am indebted to the collectors of children's games: Alice Gomme,
William Newell, Jessie Bancroft, Leslie Daiken, Norman Douglas,
Brian Sutton-Smith, Dorothy Howard, Edith Fowke, Iona and Peter
Opie and many others.

My thanks go to the staff of the Osborne Collection of Early
Children's Books, Toronto Public Library, and the staff of the
Museum and Archive of Games at the University of Waterloo. Thank
you also to my family who played with me, to my friends who
helped me remember how we played, and to Dušan for sharing his
idea with me. – C. G.

Pssst! Thank you Trudee.

CONTENTS

INTRODUCTION

People have been playing games for thousands of years. Games have been played in different ways in other times and places, but the patterns are always the same.
We love to jump and hop, throw and catch, chase and hide.

Many playthings are found in nature. We play with twigs and leaves, pebbles or stones, small bones, nuts and shells.

Other playthings are borrowed. Buttons, bottlecaps, rings and thimbles all become part of our games. Games like Tag are played without anything at all.

Most of the games in this book are hundreds of years old. Some games like Jackstones and Hide and Seek go back to the ancient Greeks and Romans.

The book tells you how each game can be played, but you and your friends can agree to change the rules. These games belong to you, too. They are yours to play.

COUNTING OUT

There are different ways to choose "It" for games like Tag and Hide and Seek. The first one who says "I'm not It" is not It! The last one to reach a tree or a fence has to be It. Or you can choose It by counting out fists, feet or first fingers using a rhyme. Some people think that nonsense counting-out rhymes like "Eeny Meeny Miny Mo" are old ways of counting. Shepherds might have used words like these to count their sheep.

You count out on the beat of the rhyme. If the pointing finger lands on you at the end of the rhyme, you are out.

<u>Two</u>, <u>four</u>, <u>six</u>, <u>eight</u>,
<u>Mary</u> <u>at</u> the <u>garden</u> <u>gate</u>,
<u>Eating</u> <u>cherries</u> <u>off</u> a <u>plate</u>,
<u>Two</u>, <u>four</u>, <u>six</u>, **eight**.

Sky blue, sky blue,
Who's it? Not you!

Intery, mintery, cutery corn,
Apple seed and apple thorn.
Wire, brier, limber lock,
Five geese in a flock.
Sit and sing by a spring,
O-U-T and in again.

Or end it this way:

Three geese in a flock.
One flew east,
and one flew west,
One flew over the
   cuckoo's nest.

Put in both fists for:

One potato, two potato,
Three potato, four,
Five potato, six potato,
Seven potato, more.

Mickey Mouse built a house.
How many bricks did he use?
"Four."
1-2-3-4 and out you must go.
Not because you're dirty,
Not because you're clean,
Just because you kissed a girl
Behind a magazine.

The last person left in will be It.

TAG

Chasing and being chased — that's what Tag is all about. In a game of Tag, It can change you with a touch. You might have to freeze until you are freed or hold on to the part of your body that It tagged, while you run. One thing is for sure — you probably won't be It for long!

Puss in the Corner

Puss in the Corner is one of the oldest of all the Tag games. It's for five players.

• Four people make a square, one at each corner. The fifth is in the middle and wants a corner too.

• The people in the corners have to change places. They can call out or signal to the person they want to change with. As they change, the person in the middle tries to run to an empty corner.

• The new person without a corner becomes Puss and stands in the middle.

• If Puss is having trouble getting a corner, he can call out "All change." Then all five people scramble for the four corners.

The Moon and the Morning Stars

When the sun shines, you can play the Moon and the Morning Stars.

• The person who is It is the moon. She must stay in the shadow of a building or a large tree.

• The morning stars stay mainly in the sun, but dance in and out of the shadow. Any star who is tagged in the shadow becomes the new moon.

Fox and Geese

Fox and Geese is a game for the snow — or the sand.

• In the snow, the players stamp out a large wheel with spokes. There is a safe place at the hub or centre of the wheel.

• The fox tries to catch the geese, who run out of the safe centre, around the wheel, and across the spokes. The fox must also stay on the paths.

• A goose who is caught changes places with the fox.

Shadow Tag

On a sunny day, try playing Shadow Tag. You are tagged when It steps on your shadow.

Frozen Tag

• When It tags other players, they must freeze on the spot. If a player was standing on one leg with his arms in the air when he was tagged, that's the way he must stay.

• Frozen people can be freed when another player touches them or — and this is harder — if someone crawls between their legs.

• The game ends when everybody is frozen. The last one frozen becomes It for the next game.

PSSST! IN TOUCH TAG, OR STICKY APPLE, YOU MUST HOLD ON TO THE SPOT WHERE YOU WERE TAGGED AS YOU RUN. TRY TO TAG PEOPLE IN PLACES THAT MAKE IT HARDER OR FUNNIER FOR THEM TO BE IT, LIKE A KNEE, AN ANKLE OR A NOSE!

FROZEN TAG

HIDE AND SEEK

All hide and spy games are played in pretty much the same way. Somebody — or a lot of somebodies — is It. Somebody — or a lot of somebodies — hides. There is a safe home base, It has to count before he comes to look, and the hiders have to race to be "home free." Hide and Seek has been called "All Hid," "Hideygo," or "Whoop," but it has been played like this for thousands of years.

Here are two ways to play.

Hide and Seek

• The person who is It covers her eyes at the spot chosen for home base. She has to count, usually to 50 or 100, while everybody scatters and hides. She shouts "100" or "Ready or not, here I come!" and sets off to search for the hiders.

• When she spies one of them, she has to call out his name and they both race towards Home.

• If she beats him Home, touches the base, and cries "One, two, three on _____," he is caught. But if he reaches home base first and calls out "One, two, three for me," or "One, two, three, home free," he is safe.

• A player doesn't have to wait until he is found to race back Home.

• When all the players are found, the first one caught becomes the new It.

Sardines

Sardines is Hide and Seek — but backwards.

• All the players cover their eyes and count while one person hides.

• Everybody looks for the hider.

• When a seeker finds the hider, he waits until nobody is near, then creeps into the hiding place with him. The seekers slowly disappear, and the hiding spot becomes more and more cramped. That's why this game is called "Sardines" or "Sardines in a Tin."

• The game is over when the last seeker finds the sardines. The first seeker to find the hiding place hides to begin a new game.

A long time ago, the hiders used to signal to the seeker that they were ready by calling out "Whoop!" or "Whoop Oh!" When just one person hid, he called "Spy All!" when he was ready.

HUNT THE THIMBLE

In the game of Hide and Seek, what is hidden is well out of sight. In Hunt the Thimble games, something small is hidden, but it's right in front of the eyes of the hunters. The trick is to find it.

Here are two different ways to play. In both, the first person to find the thimble hides it the next time.

Here's a tip: Hide your "thimble" near something that is the same colour.

Hot Buttered Beans

• The players wait in another room while one person hides the thimble or other small object. It must be in full view.

• She calls out, "Hot buttered beans! Please come to supper."

• As the other players look for the thimble, she lets them know when they are near. They are cool or freezing when they are far away; as they get closer, they are warm, getting warmer, burning hot!

• Sometimes, just one person leaves the room while everybody else hides the thimble.

Huckle Buckle Beanstalk

• One person hides the thimble in full view.

• The other players hunt for the thimble as usual. As each one finds it, he quietly says, "Huckle Buckle Beanstalk," and sits down. He doesn't look at the thimble, of course.

• The game goes on until everybody has found the thimble or until the hider says the game is over.

LEAPFROG

Leapfrog is one of many hopping, leaping and jumping games. It can be played by two friends on their way somewhere, or by many friends to warm up on a chilly morning.

The *Little Pretty Pocket Book* was written for children in 1744. Here is its Leapfrog poem:

This stoops down his Head,
Whilst that springs up high;
But then you will find,
He'll stoop by and by.

That's how two friends play Leapfrog. One friend bends over to make a "back," then the other leaps over him. When the leaper bends over, it is the back's turn to jump.

Tips for backs

• You can make a "little back" on your hands and knees. Tuck in your head.

• You make a "low back" by bending over and grabbing your ankles, or by resting your elbows on your knees.

• When you put your hands on your knees, you make a "high back."

• Always tuck your head in, and stand still and solid.

Tips for leapers

• When you jump, put your hands down flat — no knuckles on the back's back.

• Only your hands touch the back as you go over him.

Hop Frog

This is a leap-frogging game in which everybody hops about.

• To turn yourself into a frog, bend over as if you are going to sit down. Now rest your hands on your knees and spring about. See who can hop for the longest time!

Leapfrog

• The players line up. The first person in the line bends over to make a back. The leaper behind him may ask for "low back" or "high back."

• The leaper jumps over the back, goes a few steps ahead, and bends over to make a back.

• The next in line jumps over these two backs one at a time, then bends over to become the third back in the line.

• When the last player in the line has jumped over all the backs, the first one starts again.

Keep the Kettle Boiling

This game is played like ordinary Leapfrog, but the players stand up to become leapers as soon as they have been leapt over. More than one person is jumping at a time, and the leaper immediately has to become a back for the person behind him.

Sending a Letter

This game comes from London, England. It was originally called Sending a Letter to Canada.

• The first player makes a back. The leaper pretends to write on his back, bang on the stamp, and mail the letter up under his jacket. Then he leaps over the back saying, "Sending a letter."

HOPSCOTCH

There are many ways to play hopping games. You can count your hops, or see who can hop the longest or the farthest. You can add a big step after your hop, and then a jump, to play Hop, Step and Jump. When you draw a pattern on the ground to hop through, you're playing Hopscotch, hopping over lines "scotched" or scratched on the ground. Some of the earliest Hopscotch patterns were probably round and looked like labyrinths or mazes.

To play the game

To play Hopscotch, you need chalk to draw your pattern. Sometimes you also need a marker to throw into each square. Hopscotch markers are often called "pucks" or "potsies." People have always used whatever is handy for a marker — a smooth flat stone, an oyster shell, a broken piece of crockery or a shoe-polish tin filled with sand or dirt.

• Draw your pattern — it may look like a snake, a snail or an airplane.

Snake Hopscotch

This pattern is just for hopping through — you don't use a marker. Hop from side to side without touching the lines, or hop up one side and down the other.

Round Hopscotch or the Snail

• Hop around the pattern. Keep your balance and try not to step on any lines. When you get to the space in the centre, you can rest there on both feet. Now hop back out.

• Each time you hop into the centre and out again without stepping on the lines or putting down your other foot, you write your initials in any square. This space is your Home. You may rest in your home space, but all the other players must hop over it.

• Each player has her own rest spaces, so the hopping can get very tricky.

PSSST! PLAY IT AT THE BEACH. JUST DRAW YOUR PATTERN IN THE SAND.

PSSST! THE HOPSCOTCH REST SPACE HAS BEEN CALLED PLUM PUDDING, HOME OR PARADISE.

Airplane Hopscotch

This pattern is much older than airplanes, but it does have wings. If you like, you can put "ears" around squares 1 and 2. When you stand in the ears, it's easier to throw your marker to the squares near the end of the pattern.

• Throw your marker into 1. Hop over 1, into 2 and then 3. Land in 4 and 5, one foot in each. Hop into 6 and land in 7 and 8 together. Square 9 is a hop, and 10 is a turn-around rest space. Land in it on two feet, turn around with a jump, then start hopping back.

• Hop all the way back to 2, bend over, pick up your marker, and hop into 1 and out of the pattern.

• The marker must always land inside the lines of each space. Don't step on any lines, and try not to fall over.

• Throw your marker into 2. Hop into 1, over 2 and keep going, hopping and landing through the pattern to the end. Turn around, hop back to 3, pick up your marker from 2, hop through 2 and 1, and out of the pattern. When your marker is in one of the landing spaces – 4 or 5, 7 or 8 – you won't be able to land on two feet: you'll have to hop through that part of the pattern.

• When you've thrown your marker to 9 (you can use the ears) and hopped all the way there to get it and then back, the game is over.

• If you are taking turns to play, you start your next turn where you stopped the last time.

Try playing the game these ways:

• Throw your marker into 1, and hop into 1 after it. Now, with your hopping foot, kick the marker into 2, then 3. You hop and kick with the same foot, so you scuffle the marker to the end of the pattern and back. You can hop and scuffle more than once in each square, but neither you nor your marker may land on any lines.

• Hop through the pattern balancing your marker on your hand, your elbow or the top of your head.

HOPSCOTCH

SKIPPING

Spring is skipping season. People used to think that jumping around in the spring would make the crops grow. They hoped that the plants would grow as high as the jumpers jumped. When skipping first became popular, it was a boy's game. Boys did tricks like turning the rope twice for one jump and skipping with crossed hands. Later, girls added the rhymes.

You can skip alone, holding the ends of a short rope. When you skip with your friends using a long rope, the people turning the rope are called "enders."

Skippers usually run in and out of the rope, but you can also stand in and start on the count of three.

Ipsey, Pipsey,
Tell me true,
Who shall I be married to?
A ... B ... C ... D ...

(Skip until you trip on a letter. It's the first letter of your future sweetheart's name!)

Skipping has its own language.

Salt (Turn the rope slowly.)

Mustard and Vinegar (Turn the rope at normal speed.)

Pepper or Peppers (This has always meant turning the rope as quickly as you can.)

Bluebells (The rope swings from side to side. It doesn't go over the skipper's head. This is also called Rocking the Cradle.)

High water (The rope doesn't touch the ground as it turns.)

Chase the fox (All the players follow the fox, doing what she does as she runs under the rope or skips once or twice.)

Under the moon (The skippers run under the rope, without skipping.)

Over the stars (The skippers jump once over the rope.)

PSSST! TRY PEELING THE APPLE. JUMP IN. JUMP ALL AROUND THE PERSON WHO "APPLE," IS SKIPPING. THE PEELED APPLE RUNS OUT AND YOU STAY IN TO BE PEELED.

House to rent,
Enquire within.
When I jump out,
Let _____ jump in.

(This is one of the oldest skipping rhymes. Call in a friend, jump a couple of times together, then jump out. Your friend stays in to call a new friend.)

Bluebells, cockleshells,
Eevy, ivy, over.
My mother sent me to the store,
And this is what she sent me for:
Salt, mustard, vinegar, pepper!

(For "pepper," the enders turn the rope as fast as they can.)

Grapes on the vine,
Ready to be picked.
One fell off,
And the other did the splits.

(Skip until "splits," then stop the rope between your legs.)

Apples, peaches, pears and plums,
Tell me when your birthday comes.
January, February, March ...
First, second, third ...

(Jump in on your birthday month, and jump out on the date.)

BALLS

Balls may be the oldest playthings. People rolled, or threw and caught, anything that was round. Later on, balls were made of strips of leather sewn together and stuffed with hair or feathers. The first ball games were games of catch, but bouncy balls and paved school yards changed the way people play with balls.

Queenie

• The player chosen to be Queenie stands with her back to the other players and throws a ball backwards over her head. The other players all try to catch it. When one has it, the players put their hands behind their backs.

• Queenie turns around and guesses who has the ball. If she is right, she is Queenie again. If she is wrong, the person who has the ball becomes Queenie.

Call Ball

You can play this game by throwing the ball up into the air or by bouncing it high against a wall.

• Each player is given a number or the name of one of the days of the week.

• The first player throws the ball and calls out a day or a number.

• The player whose day or number is called has to run and catch the ball before it bounces more than once.

• If he catches the ball, he calls next. If he misses, the first player throws and calls again.

Four Square

This is a game for four players and a line of people waiting for a turn. Use a rubber ball you can bounce with two hands.

• Draw a big square on the ground and divide it up into four smaller squares. Each person stands in a small square.

• Choose a subject: colours, animals, names of boys or girls, provinces or movies.

• The player with the ball calls out a colour, for example, or a name, and bounces the ball into any other square.

• The person standing in that square catches the ball, then does the same. The ball bounces from square to square. The players may not repeat any words.

• If someone misses a catch or can't think of a word, the next player waiting in line steps into his square. The new player can dash in to try to keep the game going, or the players can choose to start a new game with a new category.

Ball bouncing

Rhymes are used for ball bouncing, skipping and clapping — you can bounce your ball instead of clapping, or skip to a ball-bouncing chant. Here are two games to try.

O'Leary is a ball-bouncing game. Bounce the ball for "One, two, three." Your leg goes over the bouncing ball each time you say "O'Leary." Catch the ball at the end.

One, two, three, O'Leary,
Four, five, six, O'Leary,
Seven, eight, nine, O'Leary,
Ten, O'Leary,
Catch me.

Ordinary Moving is a wall-ball game. You throw the ball against the wall, then do something before you catch it. Or you might have to catch the ball in a certain way. You can let the ball bounce once. Chant the words as you throw and catch.

Ordinary *(Throw the ball and catch it.)*

Moving *(Throw the ball and catch it without moving your feet.)*

Laughing *(Throw and catch the ball. Keep a straight face.)*

Talking *(Throw the ball, touch your mouth, then catch the ball.)*

One hand *(Throw and catch with one hand.)*

The other hand *(Throw and catch with the other hand.)*

One foot *(Throw and catch while standing on one foot.)*

The other foot *(Throw and catch while standing on the other foot.)*

Clap front *(Throw, clap your hands, and catch the ball.)*

Clap back *(Throw, clap behind your back, and catch the ball.)*

Front and back *(Throw, clap in front, then behind your back, and catch the ball.)*

Back and front *(Throw, clap behind your back, then in front, and catch the ball.)*

Tweedles *(Throw, twirl your hands around each other one way, and catch the ball.)*

Twidles *(Throw, twirl your hands around each other the other way, and catch the ball.)*

And away she goes *(Throw, spin around, and catch the ball.)*

If you can do all this without dropping the ball, try going through the whole chant throwing and catching the ball without moving. *(When you come to "One foot" and "The other foot" just touch them. And wave your arms around for "Away she goes.")* Then you can try keeping a straight face through the whole chant, or touching your mouth, and so on. You could be busy all day!

PSSST! TRY BOUNCING YOUR BALL TO ONE, TWO, BUCKLE MY SHOE.

CLAPPING GAMES

"Pease Porridge Hot" was one of the first clapping rhymes. People used it on wintery mornings to warm up their hands. Perhaps that's why one of the names for this game is Hot Hands. It's easy to get mixed up, and you have to think hard to keep up with your partner. But the faster you play, the better.

There are lots of ways to clap. Here are some of them.

• Clap your hands on your legs.

• Clap your own hands together.

• Clap your friend's hands:

Clap both hands straight on, nothing fancy.

You and your friend clap right hands, clap your own hands, then clap left hands.

You and your friend clap the backs of each other's hands, turn your hands, then clap straight on.

Turn your hands so that one palm faces up towards the sky and one faces down towards the ground. Your friend does the same. Your sky hand claps her ground hand, and your ground hand claps her sky hand. Now flip each hand over and do it again.

• Cross your hands on your chest between claps.

Start with this clap for "Pease Porridge Hot." Clap the same pattern for each line.

Pease porridge hot,

(Clap your hands on your legs, clap your own hands, clap your friend's hands.)

Pease porridge cold,
Pease porridge in the pot,
Nine days old.
Some like it hot,
Some like it cold,
Some like it in the pot,
Nine days old.

PSSST! YOU CAN CLAP TO ANYTHING. TRY OTHER NURSERY RHYMES, ADVERTISEMENTS, YOUR FAVOURITE SONG OR A WORD LIKE MISSISSIPPI!

Use this longer clapping pattern for each line of "A Sailor Went to Sea."

A sailor went to sea, sea, sea,

(Clap your own hands, clap right hands, clap your own hands, clap left hands, clap your own hands, clap straight on three times.)

To see what he could see, see, see,
But all that he could see, see, see,
Was the bottom of the deep blue
    sea, sea, sea.

Follow the clapping pattern through "When Johnny Was One."

When Johnny was one,
He learned to suck his thumb,

(Clap own hands, clap straight on, clap own hands, clap right hands, clap own hands, clap left hands, clap own hands, clap straight on.)

(Clap own hands.)

Thumbdoodle, thumbdoodle,

(Clap right hands, clap own hands, clap left hands, clap own hands)

Half past one.

(Cross hands on chest, clap on legs, clap straight on.)

When Johnny was two,
He learned to tie his shoe,
Thumbdoodle, thumbdoodle,
Half past two.

When Johnny was three,
He learned to climb a tree.

... four, he learned to shut the door.

... five, he learned to take a dive.

... six, he learned to pick up sticks.

... seven, he learned to go to heaven.

... eight, he learned to shut the gate.

... nine, he learned to tell the time.

... ten, he learned to feed the hens.

When Johnny was ... Goodbye!

HAND GAMES

Flashing Fingers was played in Egypt four thousand years ago and it's still being played today. Whether you're playing a game with hand shapes, making a tall pile of hands, or wiggle-waggling your thumbs, your hands are the "handiest" playthings.

Hands on Hands

This game is fun to play with lots of people.

• Gather around a table or other flat surface for the game. The first player puts his hand on the table with the palm facing down. Now each player in turn adds one hand to the stack. When each player has put in one hand, the players go around the circle again. This time each player puts in his other hand.

• When the pile is finished, the players pull their hands out, one by one, from the bottom of the pile and put them on top of the stack.

Flashing Fingers

Here's how to "flash" your fingers. Shake your closed hand twice, then flash out your fingers on the count of three.

There are different ways to play this game.

• One player flashes out a number of fingers on one hand, and the other player guesses how many. The finger flasher and the guesser both use the three count. They must flash and guess at exactly the same time.

• Two players flash fingers on the count of three. At the same time, each player calls out the number of fingers she thinks the other player will flash.

• Two players play together. Each one flashes fingers and calls out her guess for *all* the fingers flashed. Each player must decide how many fingers she will flash (from one to five), guess how many her friend will flash (from one to five), and then figure out what the total will be.

PSSST! SCISSORS, PAPER, STONE CAN ALSO BE USED TO CHOOSE IT.

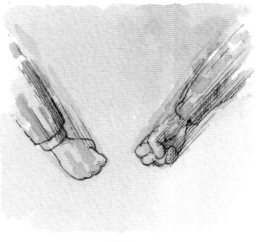

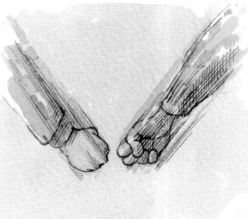

Scissors, Paper, Stone

In this game, you flash hand shapes. In each pair of shapes there is a winner.

- Make scissors with your index and middle fingers.
- Paper is a flat hand, palm facing down.
- Stone is a closed fist.

- Scissors cut paper, so they win.

- Paper covers stone, so it wins.

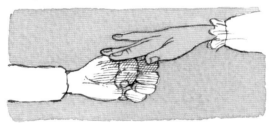

- Stone can dull scissors, so it wins.

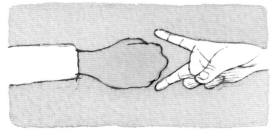

  If you both flash the same shape, try again.

Wiggle-Waggle

Wiggle-Waggle is Simon Says with thumbs.

- To play, make your hands into fists and stick your thumbs out.
- When Simon calls "Simon says thumbs up," stick your thumbs up.
- When Simon says thumbs down, turn your hands so that your thumbs point down.
- When Simon says Wiggle-waggle, wiggle your thumbs.
- Don't do any of these unless "Simon says ..."

HAND SHADOWS

Shadows on the wall — funny, spooky or beautiful. They're magical because they look so different from the hands that make them.

Here are some tips for shadow makers.

• Use a small light source like a reading lamp or a flashlight. The light bulb should be clear, not frosty. Frosty bulbs are for people who don't want shadows.

• For a screen, use a bare wall that's a light colour, or tape up a piece of white paper.

• Sit or stand between the light and the wall. The light, you, and the screen must be in a straight line.

• Move yourself or move the light until you get dark shadows with clear outlines.

• Don't look at your hands, look at the shadows you are making.

Now try making some shadow pictures.

Duck

Elephant

Cow

Bird

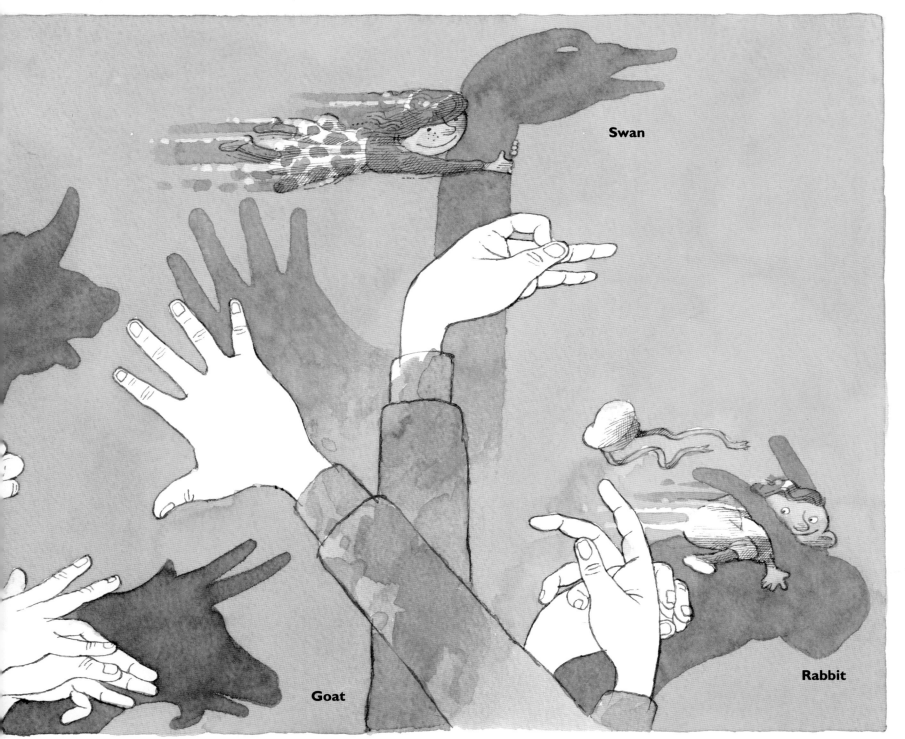

Swan

Goat

Rabbit

35

BROKEN TELEPHONE

If you had played this game a hundred years ago, you would have called it Russian Scandal. Now we call it Gossip, Broken Telephone or Whispers Down the Lane.

It's easy to play. All you need is a group of friends with ears!

• The players sit in a circle or a row.

• The first player whispers something, just once, to his neighbour — a phrase or a sentence.

• The neighbour whispers what she heard — or thinks she heard — to the person next to her.

• The message is passed on from player to player. The last person to hear the message repeats it out loud. The message will get funnier and odder as it is passed along.

JACKSTONES

In ancient Greece and Rome, this game was called Astragals because it was played with the astragalus or ankle bone of a sheep. Players threw five "knucklebones" up into the air and tried to catch them on the backs of their hands. The same throwing and catching game is played with five stones, five shells, little silk beanbags filled with rice, or jacks and a ball.

Jacks

Jacks are small metal shapes that are used instead of real knucklebones. They are easy to pick up because they sit on only three of their six legs. The game is played with five or ten of these jacks and a small rubber ball.

You can throw the ball up and let it bounce once before you catch it, or you can bounce it down, let it bounce up, and then catch it. See which way you like best.

Here are some ways to play with five jacks and a ball.

Scatters

• Scatter your jacks on the ground.

• Oneseys: Throw the ball, pick up one jack, then catch the ball with the same hand. Put the jack in your other hand. Throw the ball again and pick up the next jack, then catch the ball. Do this until you have picked up all the jacks one by one.

• Twoseys: This time you pick up the jacks two at a time. Look at the scattered jacks and choose carefully which two you will scoop up together each time. If you are just starting, "Dubs" might be allowed — you may arrange the jacks before you try to pick them up.

Throw the ball, pick up two jacks, catch the ball. Put the jacks in your other hand. Throw the ball and pick up two more jacks, then catch the ball. Put these two jacks into your other hand as well. Throw the ball, pick up the last jack, then catch the ball.

• Threeseys: Pick up three jacks on your first throw, then two on your second. Now it's even more important to choose which jacks you will scoop up together each time.

- **Fourseys:** Throw the ball, scoop up four jacks, then catch the ball. Pick up the last jack on your next throw.

- **Fiveseys:** Scatter the jacks, but not too far apart. Throw the ball and scoop up all the jacks before you catch it.

PSSST! WITH STONES, THREESEYS IS ALSO CALLED THE HORSE AND CART. THE THREE STONES ARE THE CART. THE SINGLE STONE IS THE HORSE.

Fivestones

Scatters can be played without a ball and with stones instead of jacks. Fivestones is a much faster game than Jacks. A bouncing ball gives you more time to pick up your playing pieces than a falling stone does.

You can collect some smooth pebbles to use for this game. They should be round enough to be picked up easily, but not so round that they roll away. Keep looking until you have five special pebbles to keep in your pocket.

Once you have scattered your stones, choose one to throw — it's called your "sky stone." Toss up your sky stone, scoop up a stone from the ground, and catch the sky stone in the same hand. Put the stone in your other hand. Pick up all the stones one by one this way.

Work your way through Twoseys, Threeseys and Fourseys just as you would with jacks and a ball. For each round, choose your sky stone carefully so that the ones you leave are the easiest to pick up together. After Fourseys, all five stones are in your hand ready to go back into your pocket.

Pigs in the Pen

This jacks game is also called Cherries in the Basket. You can play it with five stones if you like.

- Scatter the jacks.

- Make a pigpen by resting the side of your hand on the ground and curving your fingers and thumb to make an opening.

- Throw the ball and push one of the "pigs" into the pigpen. Catch the ball. One by one, push all the other pigs into the pen. You can try pushing them into the pen two by two as well.

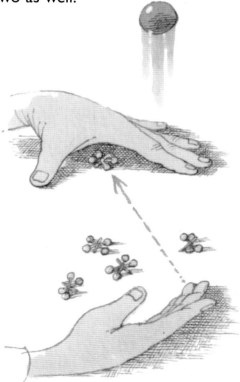

Horses in the Stable

You can play this game with jacks and a ball or with five stones.

• Make a stable for your "horses" by spreading out your fingers and thumb, and resting your fingertips on the ground.

• Put one jack into each of the four "doorways." The jacks stay near the tips of your fingers and thumb.

• Throw the ball and push one of the horses into the stable. Keep throwing the ball and pushing the horses into the stable one by one until all four jacks are inside your hand.

• Throw the ball one last time and scoop up all four horses.

Sweep the Floor

This is a game for five stones, but you can use jacks and a ball.

• Scatter the stones.

• Throw the sky stone and, with your fingertips, sweep one of the stones nearer to the others. Catch the sky stone.

• Throw the sky stone again and use your fingertips to sweep another stone closer to the others. Catch the stone. Do this until you have swept all the stones together.

• Throw the sky stone one more time and pick up all the other stones.

PSSST! TRY PEACH PITS.

Danger

Here's one last game. It's for stones or jacks without the ball, and it's difficult — so it's a game to grow on. See how far you can get.

• Scatter your stones.

• Throw your sky stone and scoop up one stone. Catch your sky stone. Now there are two stones in your hand.

• Throw two stones, scoop up a stone from the ground, and catch the two stones as they fall. Now you have three stones in your hand.

• Try to throw three stones, scoop up the fourth, and catch the three. If you line up the three stones along the palm of your hand before you throw them, they have a better chance of falling down together.

• The game ends when you manage to throw up four stones, scoop up the last stone, and end with five stones in your hand.

MARBLES

Marrididdles, cat's eyes and taws — marbles have their own language. Marrididdles are homemade marbles made of clay and left to dry in the sun. Cat's eyes are glass marbles with swirls of colour inside. And a taw? That's another name for the favourite marble you keep to shoot with.

Long before there were marbles, people rolled smooth pebbles or built little pyramids of nuts and tried to knock them down. Early marbles were made of stone or clay, but they've also been made of wood, steel, agate and other semi-precious stones, and glass. Looking at the patterns inside the little glass balls is one of the delights of marbles.

But marbles are to be played with, not just looked at. You can choose to play for fun — you get your marbles back at the end of the game — or for keeps. You and your friends should agree which way to play before you begin the game.

You can roll, toss or shoot a marble.

To shoot a marble

• Curl your fingers. Put your thumb nail behind your index finger. Practise flicking it forward, out from behind your index finger. It's that flick that shoots the marble.

• Rest the marble in the little space made by your curled index finger and your thumb. You can curl your index finger a little more to hold the marble there.

• Now "knuckle down" – rest the knuckle of your index finger on the ground. Flick your thumb and send your marble flying along the ground.

Hits and Spans

You and a friend can play this marble chase game when you are going somewhere together.

• The first player shoots her marble.

• The second player shoots her marble, trying to hit the first marble or to come within a span of it. (You "span" two marbles by spreading out your index finger and thumb. You should be able to touch both marbles at the same time.) If she does, she wins the marble. If she doesn't, she leaves her marble there and her friend has a chance to shoot at it.

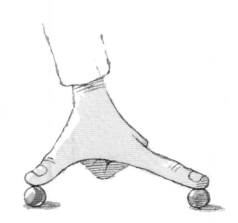

• The winner — the person who hits or spans her friend's marble — starts the game again. Of course, you could use the same two marbles over and over.

Plum Pudding or Picking Plums

• Each player puts a number of marbles on a line.

• The players take turns shooting at the marbles. A player wins the ones he knocks off the line. If he misses, he has to wait his turn to play again.

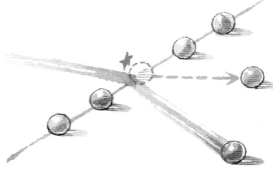

The Ring Game

Draw a ring on the ground or use a ring you find lying around, like a circular pattern in the carpet.

• Each player puts a number of marbles into the ring.

• The players agree to a starting line a little distance away from the ring. To see who will go first, each player shoots a marble from the starting line towards the ring. The player whose marble is closest to the ring will shoot first, followed by the player whose marble is the next closest. The players pick up their marbles to use as shooters for the game.

• To begin the game, the first player knuckles down at the starting line and shoots, trying to hit a marble out of the ring.

• If a player knocks a marble out of the ring and his shooter goes out too, he gets to keep the marble and he takes another turn. This time he shoots from where his shooter lies.

• If a player knocks a marble out of the ring but his shooter is left inside, he can get it back by putting a marble into the ring in its place. He is out of the game and must put the marbles he has won back into the ring.

• If a player misses and his shooter stays inside the ring, he can put a marble into the ring to get it back. He is out until the next game.

• If a player misses and his shooter rolls outside the ring, it stays there until his next turn. Then he will shoot from where his shooter lies.

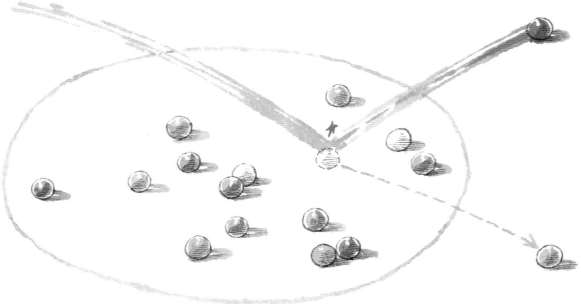

MARBLES

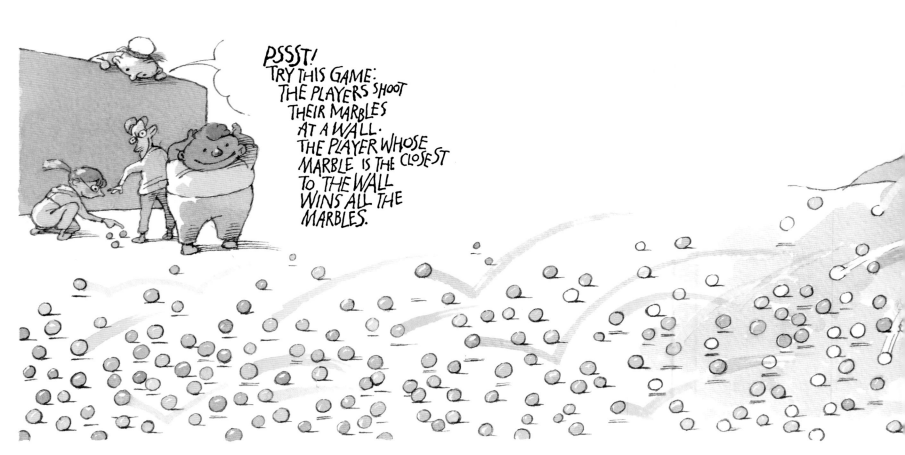

PSSST!
TRY THIS GAME:
THE PLAYERS SHOOT
THEIR MARBLES
AT A WALL.
THE PLAYER WHOSE
MARBLE IS THE CLOSEST
TO THE WALL
WINS ALL THE
MARBLES.

The artwork in this book was rendered in watercolour and pen and ink on 140 lb
Bockingford watercolour paper.

Text is set in Gill Sans
Hand lettering done by the artist

Printed and bound in Hong Kong by Wing King Tong Company Limited